D0874122

THE CLYDE PUFFER

Dan McDonald

DAVID & CHARLES
Newton Abbot   London   North Pomfret (Vt)

ISBN 0 7153 7443 5
Library of Congress Catalog Card Number: 77–076092

© DAVID & CHARLES 1977

First published 1977
Second impression 1978
Third impression 1980

Printed in Great Britain by
Ebenezer Baylis and Son Limited,
The Trinity Press, Worcester, and London
for David & Charles (Publishers) Limited
Brunel House Newton Abbot Devon

Published in the United States of America
by David & Charles Inc
North Pomfret Vermont 05053 USA

PREFACE

Scottish parents have a phrase for it—*boat daft*. It is a mental state easily contracted by a boy born and brought up, as I was, within half a mile of the once busy quays of the River Clyde in Glasgow. In these surroundings I acquired a schoolboy fascination for small craft, and it has never left me. Much of my interest was centred in the puffers. I used to watch the little vessels from the shore in Arran trailing their black ribbons of smoke low over the sea on their way to Campbeltown or the Mull of Kintyre, and I would wish that I was on board. Many years were to pass before that wish came true.

Over the years I have collected information on the puffer tribe, not with any idea of writing a book, but merely as a personal interest. As a result of giving talks about the puffers to maritime and local history societies I have been urged to write about them.

In my researches I have been assisted by numerous friends of whom I would specially mention the late Captain George Hamilton of Brodick, Messrs James Wilson, William K Work, David Burrell and Graham E Langmuir. John Thomas has given invaluable help in putting the book together. Thanks are especially due to Mr Colin McPhail and the management of Glenlight Shipping Limited for according me the privilege of making an occasional passage in their vessels and last, but not least, to my erstwhile shipmates who put up so cheerfully with the landsman in their midst.

DAN MCDONALD
Glasgow, December 1976

(Photographs are by the author unless stated otherwise)

Frontispiece and front cover: The *Turk*, built by John Hay
& Sons in 1929 sets out from Yorkhill for her day's work on
the river taking bunker coal to the dredgers and their atten-
dant hopper barges.

INTRODUCTION

Basically, the Clyde puffer was a sturdy steam coaster 66ft long, which could carry 100 tons of cargo and deliver it with her own gear wherever there was enough water to float her. Where there was not enough water she could beach herself, unload her cargo and sail away on the next tide. The early vessels of the type had non-condensing engines, the exhaust being turned into the funnel, and the resulting sound caused them to be termed 'puffers'. And 'puffers' their successors remained.

The puffer's dimensions were dictated by the size of the 70ft locks on the Forth & Clyde Canal, on which waterway many of the boats were built and through or on which they traded. There were eventually three types: the canal puffer, the estuary or 'shorehead' type, which was a development of the first, and the 'outside' boat which was sea-going.

There must be many who have heard of Para Handy, hero of Neil Munro's stories and skipper of the puffer *Vital Spark*, made known to a wide audience through the medium of television. Munro set his imaginary puffer against a background of his native Loch Fyne, but the real puffer suffered no such restrictions. She could be found in the remotest corners of the Hebrides and on the North Irish coast as far west as Donegal. The distilleries of Campbeltown and Islay obtained their barley from Kincardineshire and it came direct by puffer via the Forth & Clyde Canal. On the East Coast the puffer could be met anywhere between the Moray Firth and Middlesbrough.

Those who had served in the sailing coasters appreciated a vessel that could be kept afloat without recourse to the pumps and where the anchor was handled by steam. But there was still discomfort and danger too, as a study of the casualty returns reveal. In the dark days of winter, navigating the North Channel or the Minch with a freeboard of seven inches was no pleasure cruise.

The outside boat carried a crew of four, but the shorehead boat made do with three. The skippers were not required to hold certificates, but all were men of experience and resource, with an unrivalled knowledge of the coast. Most of them had served as enginemen at some time in their progression to command. They depended on their personal qualities to keep their crews together for there was no room for acrimony in a puffer. The enginemen, or 'chiefs' as they were usually known, seldom had paper qualifications, but it took an intelligent and capable man to keep even a small steam plant functioning properly. In the conditions prevailing in a puffer at sea a cast iron stomach was a more valuable asset than a Board of Trade certificate. The mate, as in all ships, was responsible for the anchors, the rigging and the maintenance of the vessel's fabric.

Crew accommodation consisted of a triangular space only 15ft across at the base forward of the hold and lit only by the hatch (when open) and a few glass bricks let into the deck. Into this confined space was fitted a large coal-fired range and water tank, four bunks in two tiers, a locker for food and crockery, a wooden stool or bench, a folding table and, right in the bows, the bosun's locker. The 'usual offices' were housed in a small erection like a watchman's hut situated either on the quarter deck or forward by the rigging. Puffermen had to provide their own food and how they fared depended on the culinary skill of the deckhand who was caterer, cook, relief engineer and seaman as required.

The puffer fraternity was a close-knit world of its own where almost everyone was an old shipmate. There were characters among them who are remembered chiefly by their nicknames—Handsome Harry Walker, Cocky Gray, Dublin Joe, Jock the Wrecker, the Sparrow and the Butcher, to name only a few. There is a type of man to whom the regimen of shop and factory is distasteful, and the way of life in puffers suited such folk. Of the puffers them-

Left: The sloop *Mary* of Glasgow in the Holy Loch in the early 1880s with a cargo of building timber from the sawmills on the Forth & Clyde Canal. This type of vessel, known to contemporary river men as a gabbart, had much in common with the Mersey and Weaver flats which were engaged in similar canal and estuary traffic. The Crinan Canal enabled them to reach the West Highlands and they can be seen in old photographs of Oban. The *Mary* is probably the vessel of 42 tons built at Bowling in 1845 and owned in Maryhill.

(Author's collection)

Right: The *Margret Dewar*, 42 tons gross, was built at Ardrossan in 1874 for Archibald Dewar of Silvercraigs near Ardrishaig. With her pointed stern and outside rudder she was a typical West Highland sailing coaster. Originally she was cutter rigged. The Argyllshire slate trade employed a number of these vessels.

selves Neil Munro, writing in 1907, remarked, 'I prize the little lighters—carriers of coal and coastal merchandise, whose broad uplifting bows, squat funnels, thick short masts and derricks mass so often in a figure that recalls old galleys on Celtic tombs'.

The Origin and Development of the Puffer

Before the advent of the steam coaster the area from the Clyde to Stornoway was served by a host of small sailing craft from the Clyde cutter-rigged smack carrying 30 tons to the schooner carrying 100 to 150 tons. Among these craft was a type officially known as a sloop, but called by the coasting man a gabbart. It was about 45 tons register and was 60ft long with a beam of 15 to 17ft and a depth of 6ft. The hull was full bodied with a good sheer, a rounded stern and an outside rudder. (A typical example, the *Mary*, is illustrated.) All these small vessels could and did use the Forth & Clyde Canal, but the gabbart was most closely associated with trade between the canal and

Clyde and Argyllshire ports. At this time the internal traffic on the canal, and on the neighbouring Monkland Canal, was carried in horse-drawn scows, the newer of which were of iron.

The stern-wheel steamer *Charlotte Dundas*, tried on the Forth & Clyde Canal in 1802, was a technical success, but she was unacceptable to the canal proprietors who feared the effect of her wash on the canal banks. Other experiments with steam followed, but the horse reigned supreme until 1856. In that year James Milne, the canal engineer, converted an iron barge into a screw steamer by installing a twin cylinder engine of $6\frac{1}{2}$in bore and 10in stroke powered by steam from a boiler 3ft in diameter. This vessel, the *Thomas*, carrying 80 tons of cargo, was put to work between Glasgow and Falkirk with such success that by 1860 there were 25 steam vessels on the canal, many conversions from barges similar to the *Thomas*.

About this time Swan & Co, lessees of Kelvin Dock on the canal at Maryhill in the north west of Glasgow, started to build small steamers specially designed for canal and river work.

These early puffers were strongly constructed of iron with a hull form borrowing something from the sailing gabbart. They were flush decked with little sheer, were without bulwarks except at the ends, and were protected by stout strakes of belting. The engine was usually a single cylinder simple type of 12in bore and 12 to 14in stroke, but sometimes a twin cylinder engine of equivalent power was used. The engine controls were on deck handy to the steersman, and this was to remain the practice as long as puffers lasted.

The sea-going puffer was developed during the 1870s. In this type all round bulwarks were fitted, and wheel steering of the barrel and chain type replaced the tiller. Raised quarter-decks were introduced giving more buoyancy and increased bunker space. Condensers came into general use. The 1880s saw the introduction of the compound engine, although some of the original engines were converted by adding a new high pressure cylinder on top of the existing one. All the seagoing puffers carried a big gaff trysail and sometimes a staysail also.

In the early 'nineties the puffer evolved into the form it was to retain until its demise 70 years later. The hull was full forward, more so than in the older vessels, but the curves of the run were quite shapely below water. There was considerable sheer, as much as 36in forward and 30in aft. Contrary to popular belief the puffer was not flat bottomed. The hull was round-bilged and had two or three inches of dead rise to allow bilge water to flow to the centre line, and it was strengthened by a bar keel four or five inches deep. (Beach cargoes usually commanded higher freight charges and insurance to cover the risk of a puffer inadvertently settling on a rock and 'putting her back up'.) The vessel had a raised quarter deck 21ft long on the level of the main rail. The steering wheel and compass were right aft and the engine controls were close at hand on the after end of the house.

The hold was 30ft long with a cargo hatch 25ft by 12ft. Coamings of 27in rose to 30in on the centre line. The winch, placed forward of the mast, had whelps fitted on the double pur-

Left: The *Fairy Dell* in the Clyde off Port Glasgow. Built at Ardrossan in 1897, she was one of the fleet of trading vessels which kept the smaller ports and creeks of the Clyde islands and Argyll supplied with coal and building materials. Two or three, including the *Fairy Dell*, survived until the outbreak of war in 1939.

(Author's collection)

chase ends to grip the anchor chain. The punt, as the 14ft lifeboat was called, was stowed on the forward part of the hatch during a sea passage. The mast was stepped in a steel tabernacle and was hinged for lowering. The discharging gear included a pair of shallow iron 5-cwt tubs, the boats engaged in sand dredging carrying a patent grab and a sand screen. Many boats were equipped with the stanchions and boarding necessary to erect a temporary bulkhead in the hold to divide separate consignments or for trimming purposes.

The typical engine was a vertical compound incorporating air, feed and circulating pumps. A common type built by Gauldie, Gillespie & Co had cylinders 11in and 22in diameter by 16in stroke working at 90 or 100lb/sq in at 120 revolutions. In some cases a single crank tandem was installed to save lateral space. Also provided was a donkey pump which fulfilled various functions, and many vessels, particularly those engaged in sand dredging used a 'blower' or steam ejector to clear the bilges of water.

The boiler usually was of the vertical type, 12ft high and 6ft in diameter, with an internal firebox 7ft high by 5ft in diameter, and having three or four 12-inch cross tubes in the upper part. The boiler was so placed that the firedoor was turned to the starboard quarter to give the

fireman room to keep his fire-irons clear of the engine. Sometimes a Cochran or other type of smoke-tube boiler was fitted, but this entailed sweeping the tubes, a messy and unpopular job. It was more efficient than the common type which emitted a profusion of black smoke punctuated by periodic flaming at the chimney head. At times the unburnt gases formed a 5ft tongue of red flame at the funnel head, and at night the pillar of fire and the eerie glow bathing the decks marked the puffer's progress.

In the outside boats a tiny cabin was provided in the stern for the skipper. About 1910, in many boats, the wheel and engine controls were moved to the top of the engine house and enclosed in a wooden bulwark. As some of the illustrations show, this developed into a fully enclosed wheelhouse.

Builders and Owners

Of the 400 or so puffers built, the majority came from yards on the Forth & Clyde Canal. At Kelvin Dock the Swan family and their successors built more than 60 puffers between the 1860s and 1921. They also had an interest in Cumming & Swan's yard at Blackhill on the Monkland Canal where puffers suitable for that canal were built. At Hamiltonhill, on the Glasgow branch of the Forth & Clyde Canal, Burrell & Sons began in 1875 to build canal puffers for their own use. They were kept busy supplying the then new type of outside boat to various owners and by 1903, when they closed down, they had built some 50 vessels.

John Hay's entry into the carrying trade resulted from his acquisition of a horse drawn barge to serve his own farm on the canalside. By the time steam came in he had built up a thriving transport business employing a large number of boats, horses and men. In 1866 the puffers *Victoria* and *Adelaide* were built for Hay, and two years later he acquired a small shipyard on the canal at Kirkintilloch where for 90 years most of the John Hay puffer fleet was built and maintained. From first to last the firm owned almost 100 puffers, 60 of which were built in the firm's own yard. Also at Kirkintil-

loch was the yard of Peter MacGregor & Sons who contributed 20 vessels to the fleet. Of the builders outside the canal Scott & Sons of Bowling were most important, being responsible for 40 vessels. The Larne Shipbuilding Company in Northern Ireland built 10 notable boats. Surprisingly, among the outside yards was Denny of Dumbarton who built the *Ailsa* and *Garmoyle* in 1904 for a family connection of the firm.

Among the early canal traders who converted to steam were the Carron Company and James Currie's Leith, Hull & Hamburg Steam Packet Company. Both operated regular services between the Forth ports and Port Dundas, Glasgow, mostly with transhipment cargo. The Carron boats were given numbers instead of

Right: The schooner *Louisa* of Campbeltown. Built in Rothesay, Isle of Bute in 1859 for a local owner, the *Louisa* of 43 registered tons makes an interesting contrast with the *Margret Dewar*. She later went to Northern Ireland where this photograph was taken.
(Author's collection)

names, while the Currie boats bore letters of the alphabet. The latter differed in machinery arrangement from other puffers in that they had a twin cylinder V-type engine powered by a small Scotch boiler placed athwartships. To give sufficient draught for the fire a tall thin funnel about 15ft long was fitted.

Another prominent fleet was that of Richard Munro. Mories, Munro & Company were coal agents and for a number of years they had the contract to carry bunker coal to the outposts of the David MacBrayne empire. The realms of the supernatural provided the names of their puffers: the *Sylph* and the *Faun* of 1875 survived the first world war.

Ross & Marshall, a combination of two established stevedoring and coal businesses in Greenock, became puffer owners in 1872 and operated a long succession of vessels whose names had the suffix *light* or *lite*. A substantial part of the firm's business was in bunkering vessels at the Tail of the Bank off Greenock and supplying fresh water from tank vessels like their well-known *Mellite*. They were also employed in laying moorings and in salvage work. Ross & Marshall had their own yard and slipway at Greenock where they rebuilt and repaired their ships. The last puffer built at the yard was the *Warlight* of 1919. A year or two

later the yard was swallowed up by the expansion of Scott & Company.

During the boom of the 1890s several newcomers entered the puffer trade. John G Frew had a number of vessels built at Hamiltonhill including the *Fairlie Glen*, *Morag Glen* and *Ashdale Glen*, but this enterprise was unlucky. After some of the boats were lost Frew concentrated on coasters of a larger type. Another unlucky owner was W H King who managed the *Macbeth*, *Macduff*, *Macrae* and others. Within a few years the *Glens* and *Macs* had passed to other owners.

Glasgow Steam Coasters Ltd, managed by Paton & Hendry, was a much more successful concern. Included in their fleet were a dozen outside type puffers such as the *Seal*, *Walrus*, *Otter* and *Narwhal*. Another owner was T P Purdie who also managed deep sea tramps. There was also Warnock & Sons of Paisley, whose vessels, besides engaging in ordinary trading activities, dredged millions of tons of sand in the Clyde estuary to bed Glasgow's paving stones.

In the opening years of this century a new puffer could be built for about £2000 and good coal was cheap. There were still level-headed men with the ambition to own their own ships. Among them were Jimmy Burrows of the at the fore end for the accommodation of the master and engineer. As the door opened directly on to the main deck the deckhouse must have been uncomfortable in bad weather. On top of the house was the wheel, binnacle and engine telegraph, the latter a novelty in puffers. The four 75ft boats, two from MacGregor and two from A Jeffrey & Company of Alloa, were brought out from the canal in two sections.

The vessels were powered by hot-bulb heavy oil engines of Scandinavian or Dutch makes, although Beardmore supplied a two-cylinder engine, probably experimental, for the *Innisbeg*. The sea speed of the boats was about seven knots, equal to the steam puffer, but they could carry 30 tons more on the same length. Established owners must have been apprehensive at the appearance of the extra cargo capacity in an already competitive market. Inexperience in the installation and operating of the unfamiliar machinery gave rise to trouble and breakdowns, a fact not perhaps unpleasing to the traditional steam men.

A sylvan scene on the Forth & Clyde Canal. The Carron Company's mineral scow No 9 built at Glasgow in 1871 and used for conveying ironstone or coal from the company's pits at Cadder to the works at Falkirk, is seen here near Cadder. Following her is the canal pleasure steamer *Gipsy Queen*.

(Graham E Langmuir)

Petrel and Malcolm Campbell of the *Jennie* and *Ormsa*. Colin McPhail, mate of the crack excursion steamer *Lord of the Isles*, obtained the *Gleannshira* in 1903 from Scott & Sons of Bowling. The pride of ownership was reflected in the standard of upkeep and the same applied to the *Invercloy* and *Rivercloy* owned by Hamilton of Brodick. In 1895 the Hamiltons laid aside a little schooner they had been operating and built themselves the wooden puffer *Glencloy* on the bank of the Brodick Burn thus laying the foundation of the firm known to generations of puffermen as the 'Cloys'.

Internal Combustion Interlude

In 1911 John M Paton of Paton & Hendry, impressed by the advantages claimed for the internal combustion engine, formed the Coasting Motor Shipping Company in Glasgow. This company boldly ordered 18 motor coasters, ten of which were puffer type. All were given names with the prefix *Innis*. The *Innisagra* was the first of six 66ft boats which came from MacGregor's yard at Kirkintilloch in 1912 and 1913. Except for their counter sterns they were similar in appearance to their steam consorts. They had a 16ft quarter deck with a deckhouse

The Puffer in Peace and War

When war broke out in August 1914 the Royal Navy had to establish new bases on the East Coast and at Scapa Flow. Many small craft were required to attend on the fighting ships and for this task the puffers were well adapted. Grangemouth was closed to commercial trading and as a result traffic on the Forth & Clyde Canal diminished. With the closure of the railway routes to the north west coast to all except military and naval freight the West Highlands and islands became more dependent than ever on the puffer. Several boats came from the Forth to help out.

The armistice in 1918 did not bring a return to normality. Some vessels which had been on war service were sold to other waters, notably the motor puffers most of which, re-engined, served their new owners for many years. Much of the East Coast trade was lost, and the motor lorry put paid to James Currie & Company's transhipment traffic on the canal. Three Currie boats were bought by Clyde owners for shore-head work. In 1921 the last two puffers to be built at Kelvin Dock were launched. In 1920 and 1921 Peter MacGregor built five sister ships, one of them for Demerara. They were to be his last puffers. In 1923 Mackie Brothers of the White Horse Distillery in Islay had the *Pibroch* built by Scott & Sons of Bowling to

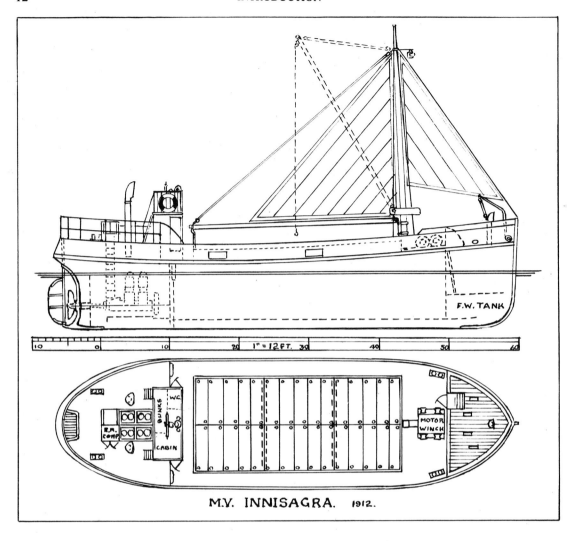

M.V. INNISAGRA.   1912.

replace a second-hand vessel they had bought in 1918.

New building between the wars was confined to replacements for vessels which were scrapped or sold. Since it was no longer essential that vessels should use the Forth & Clyde Canal, the *Glencloy* and *Sealight* built in 1930 were longer than the standard puffer, but they could be accommodated in the locks of the Crinan Canal. Welcome amenities such as wheelhouses and electric light made an appearance here and there.

The last puffers built before the outbreak of World War II were the *Anzac* and *Lascar* both for the John Hay fleet. Turned out by Scott & Sons of Bowling in 1939 they had a much deeper counter than usual and a wider cargo hatch. They were to win a place in history, for

Above: The *Innisagra* was the first of the fleet of motor vessels built for the Coasting Motor Shipping Co by Peter MacGregor at Kirkintilloch in 1912. After the dispersal of the fleet she became the property of the African and Eastern Trade Corporation of Liverpool.

(Drawing by D G Bennet)

Top right: The *Albert* a flush-decked canal type puffer built at Kirkintilloch in 1886 by John Hay & Sons for their own use. She is shown here at Bowling about 1951 in use as a coal hulk after the removal of her machinery. Note the low hatch coamings typical of the canal type puffer.

Right: The 99-ton puffer *Ardfern* was built at Kirkintilloch by Peter MacGregor & Co in 1910. She survived several strandings and sinkings and had a long and successful career. When this photograph was taken she was employed by Warnock Brothers of Paisley, mainly on sand dredging in the Clyde. She was broken up at Dalmuir in 1966.

Right: The *Lady of the Lake* was built at Bowling by Scott & Sons in 1877. In 1900 she was lengthened to 80ft. She was well known in Loch Sunart and the Sound of Mull together with her consort, the *Inchmurren*, a very similar craft.

(Graham E Langmuir)

Left: The *Kelpie*, an early seagoing puffer built at Whiteinch on the Clyde in 1868 was photographed at Maryhill. Note the conical roof to the boiler casing, the gaff trysail and the lack of sheer compared with later vessels. She was driven ashore in Arran and, after being refloated was sold to Irish owners.

(Author's collection)

the Ministry of War Transport adopted the design as the prototype of a new fleet of puffers for war service. These were the VIC craft of which 54 steam vessels and nine diesel were built. Except for two which came from Hay's yard at Kirkintilloch all were built at Thorne near Doncaster, Northwich on the Weaver and at Goole and Hull. They had compound engines with cylinders $10\frac{1}{2}$in and 22in diameter by 14in stroke, the low pressure valve of which was on the starboard side of the cylinder and driven by a rocking lever. Many of the VIC craft were carried to overseas bases on the decks of heavy lift BEL ships to serve as water

and store carriers. In 1944–5 the Ministry of War Transport built a second series of VICs. They were 80ft vessels on the straight frame principle and bore little or no resemblance to the traditional Clyde puffer. After the war Clyde owners bought more than a dozen VIC craft of the first series.

The Twilight Years

By the late 1940s the rising cost of coal and increasing wages were making the steam puffer an uneconomical proposition. Hamilton and

McPhail, who had joined forces in 1948, converted the *Invercloy* to oil firing, and Hay & Sons followed suit with the *Tuscan*. This, however, did not solve the problem. In 1953 Hamilton & McPhail had the *Glenshira* built at Bowling, the first motor puffer to be ordered for Clyde owners since Paton's experiment 40 years before. She set a new standard in crew accommodation. All hands were quartered aft with the master and engineer in individual cabins, and amenities included a galley, messroom and bath. She could carry up to 180 tons, and a five cylinder Polar diesel engine gave her a speed of nine knots which put her in the motor coaster class.

In 1959 John Hay & Sons started converting their four best puffers to diesel propulsion and scrapping the others. In 1963 the firm joined with Hamilton & McPhail to become Hay, Hamilton Ltd. Meanwhile, Ross & Marshall, who had caused some surprise by adding two new coal burners, the *Moonlight* and *Stormlight*, to their fleet in 1952 and 1957, had come under the control of the Clyde Shipping Company.

In 1967 the *Invercloy*, the last 66ft steam puffer in general trade was broken up at Dalmuir, and in the same month the *Glenholm*, ex-*Glencloy*, was wrecked at Cove, Loch Long. In the following year there was an amalgamation of the remaining puffer fleets under the management of Glenlight Shipping Ltd, and the smaller boats were gradually phased out. At the time of writing only two puffers, the diesel engined *Spartan* and *Lady Morven*, are retained as part of a fleet of modern motor coasters.

It is still possible, however, to smell coal smoke and hear the beat of a puffer's engine. In 1969 Sir James Miller, a former Lord Provost of Edinburgh, purchased *VIC 27* a fleet auxiliary water tanker, and converted her into a holiday ship mainly for the use of youth clubs. Renamed *Auld Reekie*, a doubly appropriate name, she is based at Oban in summer and usually at Inverness in winter. Another interesting survival is the *Basuto* a canal puffer built at Port Dundas in 1902. After World War I she was sold and served for a time as a sand barge. Eventually she was acquired by the Manchester Dry Docks Company for employment as a work boat. Fitted with a new engine and boiler and a heavy derrick she is still filling this useful role.

A VOYAGE IN THE *GLENCLOY*

A Personal Reminiscence

I shouldn't have been aboard the *Glencloy* at all. Mr Colin Macphail had arranged for me to make a trip in the new diesel-engined *Glenshira* to compare her modern equipment and crew amenities with those of the old-fashioned coal-burners which had changed little in 60 years, except for the addition of wheelhouses and electric light. But skipper Dan McFadyen of the *Glenshira* had got ahead of his schedule and had sailed for Lochmaddy on the day before I was due to start my holiday. However, the *Glencloy* was to load on Saturday morning for Lochboisdale in South Uist and I was invited to sail with her skipper Bill Heath.

The *Glencloy*, the second of the name, was built in 1930 by Messrs Scott & Sons of Bowling for G & G Hamilton of Brodick. She had a gross tonnage of 138 and a net tonnage of 66. Her overall length was 83.8ft, beam 19.6ft and draught 8.9ft. She had a quarter deck of 24ft, her hold was 42ft long and her single hatch was 35ft by 12ft. Her 168 horse power two-cylinder compound engine by Gauldie, Gillespie and Company of Glasgow had cylinders of $11\frac{1}{2}$ and 24in diameter and 18in stroke. Steam was supplied from a Cochran boiler.

Bill Heath was slightly built and wiry and had been in puffers most of his life. He had a cheerful outlook on life and was completely unflappable. 'Mind, it's a bit rough and ready,' he cautioned. 'Have ye ever sailed in puffers before?' I assured him I had. 'Och well,' he said, 'ye know what you're comin' to then.' As one would say, 'your blood be on your head.' That August Saturday forenoon was grey with low cloud overhead. I had found my ship beside a coal conveyor at General Terminus Quay in the heart of Glasgow, loaded, bunkered and ready for sea and still dripping from the washing down process. We were bound round the

Mull of Kintyre and up to South Uist with 155 tons of large anthracite for the seaweed plant on the island. Our movements after that would be anybody's guess.

From the presence of a long ladder on the quay I surmised that part of the crew was still ashore. In a few minutes Skipper Bill and a young lad appeared bearing an assortment of ship's chandlery and a cardboard carton of groceries and vegetables. We descended to the deck and I was introduced to Neil McVicar the cook who bore away the carton with the remark, 'The tatties is on.' 'Right,' said Bill, 'come on aft and I'll show you your quarters.' A door at the after end of the deckhouse revealed a trunk-way from which a ladder descended steeply into the skipper's cabin in the tail-cut of the vessel. On each side was a wide bunk with a drawer beneath and below that a leather-cushioned seat locker. Further aft where the cabin narrowed were two hanging wardrobes and a small table. I remarked that everything looked very snug. 'There's nothing like it in any o' the other puffers,' confided Bill. 'Old George Hamilton wasna married, and the boat was home to him. You take that port bunk. Neil has clean sheets somewhere.'

We just had time to shift into old clothes when a 'postman's knock' sounded by the cook's poker on the foc'sle bulkhead was heard all over the ship. It was the pufferman's dinner gong. At the foc'sle hatch we were met by an ascending blast of heat from the cooking stove and an overpowering aroma of fried onions. (No puffer was properly victualled without a copious supply of onions.) While Neil was dishing up the sausage and mash I had an opportunity to take stock of my surroundings.

On the *Glencloy*, being nearly 20ft longer than the standard boat, the foc'sle was larger

The *Glencloy* leaving Campbeltown Loch in company with Ross & Marshall's *Sealight* of 1930. The mate can be seen sealing the bunker lids with hard grease in case there is a rough sea on the Mull. Both vessels were in Government service at Scapa Flow from 1939 to 1946.

than usual, but followed the normal arrangement. On the port side were two pairs of bunks with seat lockers in front. Up forward was a triangular table and just abaft it a stout steel stanchion supported the weight of the winch on the deck above. Beyond the stove, against the after bulkhead, was a feature that was the talk of the puffer fraternity when the vessel first came out—a giant four-decker chest of drawers standing nearly 6ft high. ('Every man has a drawer for his clothes' was the boast.) What was kept in the lower three drawers I never discovered, but Neil kept the ship's supply of loaves in the top one.

In puffers everybody dined (if that is not too grand a word) at the captain's table. I thought I detected a touch of class distinction when the skipper and the passenger were provided with tea cups (no saucers in puffers) while the rest of the ship's company had to make do with mugs. In the course of conversation it emerged that we were a hand short. The mate was on holiday and as the skipper had refused the proffered relief young Andy had been made up to mate for the voyage. Andy was the fireman. Willie the chief, a dark-haired stalwart, did not appear to be too worried about the loss of his henchman.

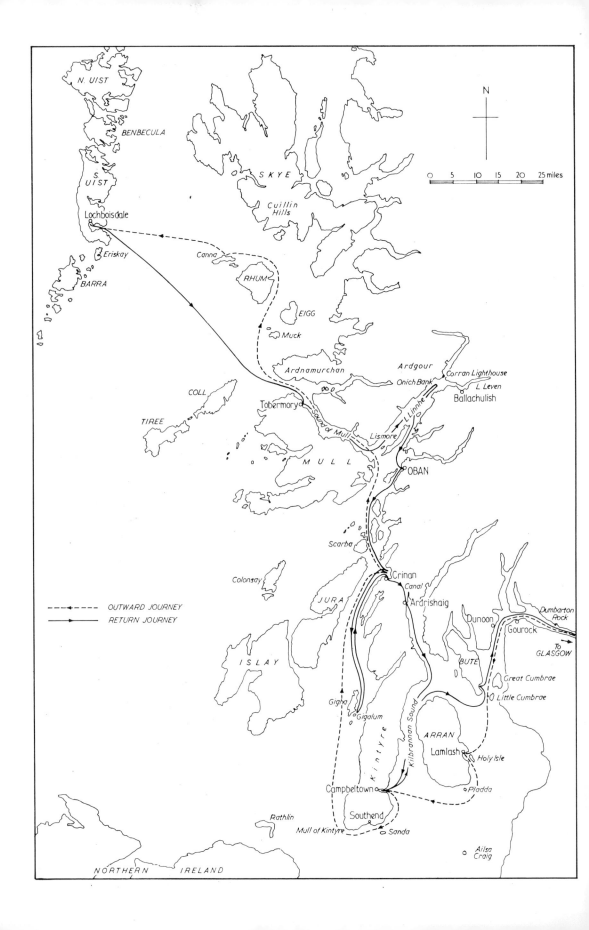

N

0 5 10 15 20 25 miles

N. UIST

BENBECULA

S UIST

Lochboisdale

Eriskay

BARRA

Canna

SKYE

Cuillin Hills

RHUM

EIGG

Muck

COLL

TIREE

Ardnamurchan

Ardgour

Onich Bank

Corran Lighthouse

L Leven

Ballachulish

Tobermory

Sound of Mull

L Linnhe

Lismore

MULL

OBAN

Scarba

Colonsay

Crinan

Canal

Ardrishaig

JURA

Dunoon

Dumbarton Rock

Gourock

To GLASGOW

BUTE

Great Cumbrae

Little Cumbrae

ISLAY

Gigha

Gigalum

Kilbrannan Sound

Kintyre

ARRAN

Lamlash

Holy Isle

Pladda

Campbeltown

Southend

Rathlin

Mull of Kintyre

Sanda

Ailsa Craig

NORTHERN IRELAND

- - - - ◄- - - - OUTWARD JOURNEY

—————► RETURN JOURNEY

At one o'clock the lone deputy harbourmaster saw us off just on high water with the whole of the tide to help us down river. We had the Clyde to ourselves. A Saturday afternoon peace hung over the normally busy shipyards and wharves. As we passed Dumbarton Rock a drizzle of rain began to smear the wheelhouse windows, and a freshening wind tossed the occasional whiff of spray over the weather bow. Presently Neil made his way over the hatch with mugs of tea for the skipper and the chief. 'There's a wee cup of tea ready doon forrit,' he informed me. On puffers the appearance of 'wee cups of tea' marked the passage of time as the striking of bells does in deep water ships. Puffer tea was strong and well laced with Ideal Milk.

Back in the draughty wheelhouse the skipper had donned his new Macintosh jumper. 'Ye would just know it was Cowal Games day,' he grunted. The Cowal Games, held at Dunoon, are seldom blessed with good weather. We sailed out of the river into the broad firth. Off Ashton, dinghy racing was in progress and we witnessed two capsizes. Motor launches were on the scene so there was no need for our attention. 'They must be gluttons for punishment,' was Bill's comment.

The wind kept freshening and occasionally both sides of the firth were blotted out by heavy rain squalls. Altogether it was a miserable afternoon. I remarked that it must have been tough in the days before wheelhouses on puffers. 'Aye, many a wet arse we got,' said Bill. 'It was murder in the winter time. An' if one hard case went out to make a passage everybody had to follow.'

By the time we were off the Cumbrae Heads the squalls out of the Arran glens were rattling the wheelhouse windows and although there wasn't much of a sea a continuous stream of rain and spray was driving across the hatch. 'Lamlash will be far enough for us the night. We'll go in and get a grip o' the railway steamer's buoy,' said Bill. By this time Arran was invisible in the murk, but during a brief clearance we got a glimpse of the entrance to Lamlash Bay. Once inside it took us several minutes of slow circling before we spotted the

Left: Map of the two-week trip on the *Glencloy* described by the author.

buoy, then young Andy nipped over the bows and stepped on to it with a rope. By the time we were secured we could see neither Arran nor the Holy Isle although both were barely half a mile away. We had been seven hours out of Glasgow, but Bill thought we should have done better since we had the tide down to the Cumbraes. It was almost dark by now and raining as hard as ever with mist right down to the masthead. The anchor lamp was set and all hands retired below to dry out.

Sunday dawned drizzling and overcast and although we lay quietly enough at the buoy the scudding clouds overhead told of wind outside. After breakfast some surplus coal on the main deck was stowed away in the bunkers and the skipper got out his fishing tackle. When after dinner one or two patches of blue sky appeared Bill was not optimistic. 'Just a flash in the pan,' he said. Nevertheless we cast off and set out for Campbeltown. By the time we rounded Pladda Island at the south end of Arran, Bill had been proved right. The ship was punching into a fresh head wind and sea, with her characteristic rockinghorse gait. After enduring four hours of this we steamed into Campbeltown Loch to find Ross & Marshall's *Sealight* at the pier. Her skipper, Willie Sutherland, dressed for going ashore took our ropes. 'Where are you bound for, Bill?' he asked. 'Lochboisdale. Where are you for?' 'Skye, Port na Long,' replied Willie. 'We should get away all right in the mornin'. The glass is up a wee bit.'

Monday morning was dry and clear and a fresh wind was blowing down the loch when, at eight o'clock, we left in company with the *Sealight*. Three hours later, at Sanda Sound, we were half a mile ahead of her which surprised Bill for *Sealight* was reputedly the faster ship. Turning west past Southend we opened up the rocky heights that reached away to the Mull of Kintyre and in no time were into the tidal turmoil off Deas Point. Even in quiet weather the sea there can jump up in heaps but that day, with the on-shore swell left over from the stormy week-end it rolled and pitched us all over the place. Two or three times we scooped up a sea over the bows, and the main deck was seldom clear of water. I could appreciate why Neil and Andy had lashed the mooring ropes to the gratings; this was no place to get a rope round the propeller. Occasionally all that could be seen of the *Sealight* was a swaying mast and a column of funnel smoke. The steady beat of the engine under our feet was reassuring, but I

Above: When puffermen spoke of 'the Mull' they meant the Mull of Kintyre. The 40 mile long Kintyre peninsula divides the Firth of Clyde from the Atlantic and 'the Mull' is at its southernmost tip. It is an area of conflicting tides and it does not take a lot of wind to raise a high, confused sea, very trying to small craft. It was no passage for the faint hearted. To avoid the worst of the tide the puffers passed close to the outlying rocks below the cliff. The pinnacle formation below the light was known to the puffermen as 'the dug's lugs'—the dog's ears. Here the *Glenfyne* is approaching the Mull of Kintyre light perched on the cliffs 300ft above the sea.

could not help wondering how the chief was faring.

In fifteen minutes we were close under the lighthouse standing high on its grassy shelf above the cliffs. We seemed uncomfortably close to the white water dashing on the black rocks at the cliff base; in fact we were no more than ten or twelve yards off the outlying rocks when we slipped safely round the Mull and steered away to the north.

For several miles we experienced a period of violent rolling in the swell setting in from the Atlantic. The wind dropped by mid-afternoon and we were abreast of the Isle of Gigha when suddenly about half a mile ahead I saw a great fish leap almost out of the water. It was at least 20ft long. 'Did you see that?' I said to Bill. 'Aye—a sailfish,' he replied unconcernedly. 'It's a bit late in the season for them here.'

We steamed steadily north and by evening a Turneresque sunset built up over Jura. Spectacular it certainly was, but Bill's verdict was that it was 'chock full o' bad weather.' At eight o'clock, with the *Sealight* for company, we turned into Loch Crinan and made fast to the pier. Any temptation to linger on deck in the twilight glow was banished by that curse of the West Coast—clouds of voracious midges. We retreated below.

I seemed to have been asleep for only minutes when I was awakened by rain drumming on the deck overhead and a loud peal of thunder reverberating round the surrounding hills. I heard no more until I became conscious of the throb of the engine and a voice saying something about breakfast. 'It's a lousy mornin',' announced Bill, 'so we just let ye lie.'

It was indeed a miserable grey morning, on

this our fourth day out of Glasgow. We had just passed Sheep Island to starboard and were heading for the Sound of Mull. Mull itself was just visible to port through sheets of heavy rain. As we made our way through the Sound, countless rain-swollen burns veined the dark Morven hills with threads of white. MacBrayne's *Lochfyne* passed us bound for Oban with a deck-load of rain soaked sheep. The puffers *Warlight* and *Polarlight* passed us in succession, salutations being exchanged from the wheelhouse windows. By two o'clock we were through the Sound and out into the wide western seas with the great granite tower of Ardnamurchan abeam and the Small Isles ahead. 'We'll go to Canna Harbour for the night,' said Bill gloomily. 'The two o'clock forecast was bad.'

During the afternoon, when we were between Eigg and Rhum, Bill brought up his binoculars. 'Must get a look at the *Jennie*. She went on the north end of Eigg last February,' he explained. All hands had a look as we passed about two miles off. There was the *Jennie* right up on a stony shore as if she had beached to discharge a cargo. 'The wheelhouse is away,' remarked someone. 'Do you see that mast stickin' out o' the water astern of her?' asked Bill. 'That's the *Lythe*,' he went on. 'She was sent up to get the coal cargo out o' her an' drove ashore.' 'They were two old Larne boats, weren't they?' I asked. 'That's right,' agreed the skipper. 'I was in one o' them, the *Petrel* before the war when the Warnocks had her. Her boiler blew up off Port Glasgow two or three years ago.'

It was coming up to eight o'clock when we anchored in Canna harbour. We were enjoying the customary 'wee cup o' tea' down forward

Below: A breezy day in the Sound of Jura, a picture taken from the deck of the *Pibroch*.

when a boat bumped alongside. The visitor, a native, was welcomed and provided with tea and a cigarette whereupon there was a general exchange of gossip concerning puffers and puffermen that had visited Canna since the *Glencloy*'s last call. Eventually our visitor got round to explaining the purpose of his call. 'I was just going off to see if I could catch a few fish,' he said, 'and I thought I would just see if you had a bag of coal to spare.' The skipper winked at Willy. 'D'ye think we could manage it, chief?' he asked. 'Aye, just give us your bag,' replied Willy. The visitor handed over his empty bag and took his leave. 'What d'ye know!' exclaimed the chief. 'There's two other bags inside this one.' 'There's nothing like a broad hint,' commented Bill. After dark our visitor returned and handed up a string of had-

docks. But he had not fished for them. 'I got them from the boat over there,' he explained indicating a group of seiners which were overhauling their nets under a blaze of decklights. After some further talk our visitor collected his coal and departed with effusive thanks.

Wednesday was dry with a fresh south-west wind, and the Cuillins of Skye stood out sharp against the morning light. We had our anchor aboard by seven o'clock and soon were steaming west under the cliffs of the north coast of Canna. But the bright morning quickly faded and it was through a grey, sloppy sea that we lurched and rolled our way across the Minch, towards South Uist with the main deck full of water. We were in Lochboisdale and had the derrick up and the hatches stripped before dinner, while the skipper went to telephone the

Below: Preparing to sail. The puffer's boat was carried on the fore part of the hatch, a rope pad being used to protect the hatch-cloth and chocks to keep the boat upright.

Above: The *Glencloy* discharging a cargo of roadstone at Inverie, Loch Nevis. Freight loaded or discharged on beaches and drying-out berths was subject to a surcharge. In 1955 the *Glencloy* was fitted for oil-burning and she was further modernised by being given a mess room, a shower cabinet and separate galley. Sold to A McNeil & Co of Greenock in 1966 she stranded at Cove, Loch Long, and shortly afterwards was broken up.

glad news of our arrival to Glasgow and to the manager of the seaweed factory on the island.

Bill recruited one of the locals to make up a quartet for the hold. Discharging started after dinner and by half past five Bill reckoned that about 40 tons of anthracite had been landed. My share in the work was confined to making the afternoon 'wee cup o' tea.'

The evening was enlivened by the arrival of MacBrayne's *Lochmor* from Oban. The arrival of a mailboat at a West Highland port is always a social occasion. The villagers gather at the pier to see the arrivals and departures. Some of them board the vessel for, according to our skipper, 'a change of drink' and a gossip.

On Thursday morning it looked as if the weather was bent on making amends. There

was bright sun, blue sky and white clouds and a cooling breeze came from the north west. We were still at breakfast when four lorries arrived on the pier to take on their loads. It seemed that every other crofter on the island owned a motor lorry, and joined in the transport business when traffic was on offer. 'You should get a lift over to the factory in the afternoon,' suggested Bill. 'There's miles of lovely sands over there —nothing between you and America. It's marvellous.' So after dinner I went out with the first load. The lorry had seen better days, and a shortage of floorboards made for a draughty drive. Since payment was made on the basis of delivered weight the lorries were piled up to the limit and a very sedate pace was maintained to prevent spillage.

The skipper was right. It *was* marvellous at the other side of the island. One had always tended to doubt the colours used by painters of Hebridean seascapes, but there they were—the emerald and blue white-capped sea, the white sands with the clouds reflected in the wet shallows and the myriads of seabirds wheeling and crying overhead. Up from the beach a few crofters were busy on the machar scything a sparse crop of oats. But time fled, and I had to get back to the ship while the lorries were still running. On arriving back at the pier I was to find that our consort the *Glenrosa* had turned up during the afternoon with a cargo of house coal from Troon.

The spell of good weather was short lived. Friday morning was overcast and the north-east wind was chilly. SS *Hebrides* came in from Glasgow on an islands cruise just as we discharged the last of our cargo. We had received orders to proceed to Onich Bank in Loch Linnhe and dredge a cargo of gravel which we were to take to the contractor who was building an extension to Gigulum pier on Gigha. At half past ten we backed out gingerly past the *Hebrides* and headed east for the Sound of Mull. On the way across the Minch, Andy and Neil removed a section of hatch covers and went down to sweep out the hold. The derrick was raised and half a tub of coal dust was tipped over the side. We had not long rounded the Hyskeir with its lonely lighthouse when a tremendous squall of hail hit us. It soon turned into heavy continuous rain which followed us into Tobermory where we tied up for the night alongside MacBrayne's *Lochinvar*. All hands turned in early, for the skipper wanted an early start next day.

It was four o'clock and still dark when the sound of the chief shaking up his fire awakened us. There was the inevitable wee cup o' tea before we slid out past the vessels conducting the current search for the Tobermory treasure and turned down a peaceful Sound of Mull in a flat calm with, at last, the promise of a fine day ahead. By the time we were in Loch Linnhe, with the morning still young, the sun was lighting the steep scarred slopes of the Morven hills and we were shearing through a sea that looked like dark green glass.

Onich Bank is the shoal that runs out from the promontory between Lochaber and Loch Leven. We stopped, hoisted out the boat and thereafter towed it astern. Bill gave me the

Right: The *Glencloy* awaits the tide at Crinan Pier. In the far distance, between Jura and Scarba, lies the Gulf of Corrievrechan. In the middle distance are the low islands which flank the Dorus Mor. The *Glencloy*, 138 tons, was one of a larger type of puffer built for G & G Hamilton of Brodick in 1930. During the second world war she served as telephone cable maintenance ship at Scapa Flow.

wheel and went down on deck to get the grab shackled on and everything ready to start dredging. When we arrived off Onich we let go the anchor, put a spring on the cable and were ready to start shortly after ten o'clock. We found ourselves in good gravel right away and the vessel was soon rolling to the weight of the grab as the winch thundered away amid clouds of exhaust steam. 'We'll have this pandemonium until we have about 50 tons aboard to steady her up,' explained the chief. Gradually the heap of gravel in the hold grew, the skipper working hard at the winch all the time for it was a job that called for muscle as well as skill. Meanwhile Andy and Neil painted our funnel its proper red colour. It had been scraped bare and oiled the day before we left Glasgow and its rusty, black appearance had invited comment during the voyage.

That was a wonderful day. We sat in the bright sunshine a gentle breeze rippling the blue water and one of the finest prospects in the West Highlands around us. Away to the west over Corran lighthouse rose the mountains of Ardgour while to the east we looked up Loch Leven to fine views of the Pap of Glencoe and other peaks beyond. Abreast of us was the slope of Lettermore where Robert Louis Stevenson's David Balfour saw the murder of the Red Fox in *Kidnapped*. Now and then we would hear a thin whistle on the shore and see a trail of white steam marking the progress of a

train along the Ballachulish branch railway.

At five o'clock Bill estimated that we had taken on 150 tons. The hatch covers were put on, the boat hoisted in and away we went for Oban taking the east side of Lismore island. It was Saturday again; we had been afloat for a week. We reached Oban just before dusk and were beaten for the last berth alongside by a fishery cruiser. Every corner was crammed with fishing boats in for the week-end so we were forced to anchor out in the bay where it is too deep for small craft to find a comfortable anchorage.

Sunday morning broke fine and sunny. The skipper rowed ashore with Andy to telephone the manager and arrange for four tons of bunker coal to be delivered at Crinan the following morning. At ten o'clock we were off to catch the tide down to Crinan. We were no further than the Fladda Narrows when we met a brisk head wind. With a six knot tide under us every sea we butted sent a sheet of spray as high as the mast head, and our newly painted funnel soon looked as if it had a coating of hoar frost.

We were in Crinan, with a relaxing afternoon and evening in front of us. The *Glenrosa* was in the canal basin and Dan Ross, her skipper, came over for a chat. He was eloquent on the shortcomings of contemporary cooks, town-bred boys especially. His last had been a willing enough lad but he had burnt every pot in the ship and thrown out the cutlery with the dish-water. As it happened our skipper had brought the *Glenrosa* up from the Thames when the firm had bought her as *VIC 29*. He related how, when he had gone alongside a string of barges to await the tide, he was asked where he was bound for. When he said 'Glasgow' the watchman replied, 'By God, Jock, you've a big heart.' The *Glenrosa* was wrecked some years later in thick weather under the cliffs of the Isle of Mull, but Dan Ross was out of her by that time.

On Monday morning our bunker coal arrived as did a crate of groceries ordered by Neil. A fine weather passage took us to Gigulum pier in about five hours. We had to use some ingenuity in securing alongside as the pier was under re-construction and had no bollards to take our ropes. With four of the contractors' men helping in the hold we unloaded 20 tons of gravel before nightfall. We went off to an anchorage for the night where Bill produced his fishing tackle again and caught a dozen or more good sized smelts which made a tasty breakfast in the morning.

Tuesday was cloudy and squally. As we continued to unload at the pier we were sheltered a bit by Cara and Gigulum islands but there was a run on the sea that made our berth uneasy. While the work went on I accompanied Bill to the island post office to pick up orders. It transpired that we were to go to Campbeltown and load coal for Glasgow.

'We could be stuck here long enough with this weather,' said Bill, and he decided to make for Campbeltown not via the Mull of Kintyre but by the Crinan Canal and Loch Fyne. Work went on all day and it was almost dark when the hold was empty. We cast off hurriedly with the derrick still aloft in an effort to get through the tricky Sound of Gigha with the last of the daylight. Having secured at sea away we went northwards rolling a bit with the wind and sea on the quarter. There was an almost full moon now, sometimes obscured by fast flying clouds and we made good time to Crinan arriving off the canal at midnight. After a long mournful blast on the whistle we drifted waiting for the lights on the sea-lock to change to green. 'Did we get ye oot o' your bed, Baldy,' said the skipper as the lock keeper took our rope. 'Aye, I was just ten minutes turned in when I heard you,' he replied.

Soon we were berthed in the basin and turned in ourselves. It had been a long day. It must have been about three o'clock when we heard a chime whistle out in the loch as another puffer sought entry to the canal. Bill, who slept with one ear open, said, 'That could be the *Sealight*.'

The *Sealight* it was. When we turned out at half past six she was lying astern of us. It was a calm, dull morning and we had one or two showers on the way to Ardrishaig. We encountered the *Invercloy* and the *Kaffir* in the canal and our skipper and Neil being local men there was chaff and gossip at every lock. After a short stay in the basin at Ardrishaig to allow Neil to forage for groceries we locked out at eleven o'clock and headed down Loch Fyne getting a wave from Warnock's *Logan* on her way to the canal. The hold was swept in preparation for the next cargo and, following an uneventful passage down almost the whole length of the Kintyre peninsula, we berthed at Campbeltown at five o'clock.

At one time Campbeltown had been a busy industrial town with some twenty distilleries, a shipyard, a coal mine and the light railway to Machrihanish on the Atlantic coast of Kintyre. Only two distilleries remained, and the coal mine after being shut for some years had recently been reopened by the National Coal Board. It was coal from this mine we were to load next morning.

Returning from an evening stroll by the loch I encountered Andy, dressed in natty sports jacket and flannels, off to sample the night life of Campbeltown.

Right: Puffers meet in the Crinan Canal. A canal meeting could be tricky especially at a bend with both boats under helm. Even in the deepest water in mid channel a loaded puffer was usually 'smelling the bottom'. Here the *Anzac* is seen approaching.

On Thursday morning it was blowing hard from the south, and the skipper, out early visiting acquaintances among the fishermen, returned with a 'fry' of fresh-caught herring and a report that the seas were 'like mountains' out in the sound. Later in the morning we took on our cargo and five tons of bunker coal. The chief looked at it dubiously. 'It doesn't get a very good name,' he said. 'But she's steamed on worse looking stuff than this.'

By mid-day the wind had eased slightly and our skipper decided 'to go out and have a look at it.' The wind had westered but a big sea was running up the Kilbrannan Sound. Bill was kept busy at the wheel as we rolled and corkscrewed over the big ones. 'They don't like a following sea,' he commented, and ground at the wheel in an attempt to anticipate the yaws, as every time the stern lifted, the rudder came half out of the water. Off Pirnmill the railway turbine steamer *Duchess of Hamilton* passed us bound for Campbeltown, lifting her forefoot out at every other sea. It was only when I tried to keep her in

the viewfinder of my camera that I realised how erratically our own small vessel was behaving in this sort of sea.

At last we came abreast of Lochranza and the bulk of Arran gave us temporary shelter before we tackled the passage to Garroch Head at the south end of Bute. We were no sooner round the Head than the wind veered to the north west and increased to near gale force sending spindrift flying across the water like smoke. Our immediate objective was Kilchattan Bay on the east side of Bute. As we approached we found one of the new railway 'Maid' class motor vessels taking the pier. As we watched, her head rope parted and she had to circle and make another approach. With the 'Maid' out of the way we made fast in torrents of rain. The engine room handrails were soon festooned with clothes drying in the heat from the boiler. We had a visit from the piermaster who just happened to be short of coal. He got two bags from our bunkers which was fair enough as we were using his pier.

The weather had quietened when at two o'clock on the Friday morning we cast off from the pier and set sail for Glasgow. There was little traffic about at that time of the day. The Burns Laird boat inward bound from Belfast overtook us off Gourock, otherwise the river was quiet. As we slipped past Erskine Ferry the crew raised the derrick and stripped the hatches. 'Berth Twenty Five' shouted the dock-master as we passed Princes Dock Tower.

And so ended a memorable fortnight when the good ship *Glencloy* had been my home. Bill accompanied me up town on his way to the office. As we parted outside the Central Station he said, 'It's a pity ye didna get better weather. But come again some time. Ye'll be welcome.'

Some years later I did have the pleasure of another trip with Bill and the chief. The ship herself was sold in 1966 and renamed *Glenholm*. In November of the following year she stranded at Cove in Loch Long and was broken up. She was the last steam puffer in regular service.

Above: The *Ashdale Glen*, 70 tons gross, was built in 1893 by Burrell & Sons at Hamiltonhill, Glasgow. She was owned in Whiting Bay, Arran, and named after a local beauty spot. This picture shows her off Ardlamont in 1926. She was broken up about 1933.

Below: The *Forward*, 57 tons, was built in 1896 at Kelvin Dock, Maryhill, for owners on the Holy Loch. This picture was taken off Port Glasgow where she had dredged a cargo of sand for herself on the sand flats off the town. After the first world war she was acquired by Rea & Company for work on the Mersey.

(Author's collection)

Above: There were many places where no shore labour was available and the puffer's crew had to discharge the cargo. Digging down through a coal cargo to get on the ceiling was a real tough job and West Highland weather was not always helpful.

Below: This photograph of the *Eisa*, taken in Kingston Dock, Glasgow, at the turn of the century shows an unusual method of getting the ship's boat out of the way. Of 92 tons the *Eisa* was built by Burrell & Sons of Hamiltonhill in 1896. She was sold to Spanish owners in 1901. Four of her consorts also were far travelled, one going to the River Plate, one to Sao Thome, one to France and another, at the ripe age of 53, to the Levant where she is reputed to have been engaged in carrying illegal immigrants to Palestine.

(Graham E Langmuir)

Above: Carron Company No 12. The Carron Company had a number of steamers in the East Coast and Continental trade from Grangemouth. This vessel, built at Port Glasgow in 1878 was employed carrying transhipment cargo along the Forth & Clyde Canal between Grangemouth and Port Dundas, Glasgow. The picture was taken on the canal near Cadder about 1905.

(John Cawley)

Below: The *Stormlight* returning from the Upper Harbour at Glasgow after discharging a cargo of granite chips from Loch Fyne. This meant negotiating five city bridges and the coasters frequenting this part of the river had to lower their masts. The *Stormlight*, of 99 tons, was built in 1933 at Port Glasgow by Ferguson Brothers for Ross & Marshall of Greenock. She was sold to the Tyne in 1952 and broken up in 1959.

Above: The *Starlight* passing Erskine Ferry on her way up to Glasgow with derrick topped up and hatches stripped ready for discharging. Of 91 tons gross she was built by Ferguson Brothers in 1937, and broken up in 1967. Her sister ship *Skylight* was sold, converted to a motor vessel and renamed *Sitka*.

Below: The *Boer* discharging coal for Lochgilphead at Miller's Bridge on the Crinan Canal. Built at Kirkintilloch in 1941 she was 72 tons gross. Together with her sister *Inca* she was hired from John Hay & Sons to feature in the film *The Maggie.* Both vessels were broken up in 1965.

Left: The *Jennie* was one of ten very similar vessels turned out by the Larne Shipbuilding Company. Of 95 tons gross she was built in 1902 for Captain Malcolm Campbell. This photograph was taken in the Kyles of Bute in 1926, by which time most puffers had had the steering gear and engine controls transferred to the top of the engine house. The *Jennie* was wrecked in 1954 on the north end of Eigg in thick weather.

Below left: The *Trojan* was built at Kirkintilloch in 1905, the *Greek*, beyond, in 1902. In their declining years these two units of the John Hay fleet were employed carrying bunker coal to the Clyde Trust dredgers and hoppers. By this time the steering wheels had been removed and tillers, guard rails and gangways fitted as on the old canal puffers. Note the throttle valve and reversing lever fitted on the casing and the binnacle-mounted skylight over the *Greek*'s engine. Both vessels were broken up in 1953.

Right: The *Druid*, 89 tons gross, second of the name, was built by John Hay & Sons in 1906, one of several powered by single crank tandem compound engines. In 1953 she was equipped with aerials for radio telephone as were many 'outside' boats. She was sold in 1955 and broken up in 1959.

Below: A group of puffers at General Terminus Quay, Glasgow. The two vessels nearest the camera are the Larne-built *Jennie* and the *Griffon*. They represent the type introduced during the 1890s and which remained almost a standard pattern until the final days of the steam-driven puffer. The large vessel in mid-stream is the *Hazelmoor* which had stranded at Ardrossan in 1920 and after being refloated was laid up at Glasgow for sale.

Above: John Hay's *Roman* loading early potatoes on the beach at Kilchattan Bay, Isle of Bute, in 1923. Of 68 tons gross she was built at Hay's Kirkintilloch yard in 1904 for the firm's canal trade. In 1913 she was given all-round bulwarks and transferred to estuary work as a 'shorehead' boat. Acquired later by the Kelso family of Corrie, Arran, she was familiar to generations of holidaymakers on that island until she went to the breakers in 1958.

Right: In 1923, after experience with two second-hand vessels, Mackie Brothers, of the White Horse Distillery, Lagavulin, Islay, had *Pibroch* built by Scott & Sons at Bowling and for 34 years she served her original owners and their successors, Scottish Malt Distillers, faithfully and well. With her well-kept appearance and White Horse weathercock at the masthead she became a familiar part of the Clyde scene on her weekly voyages to Islay. She was replaced by a motor vessel in 1957 and when sold was renamed *Texa*. Later she became *Cumbrae Lass*, a name she retained until broken up in 1967. This photograph, taken as *Pibroch* was passing Queen's Dock, Glasgow, gives a clear impression of the general arrangement of the Clyde puffer.

Below: Business and pleasure combine at Crinan as the *Pibroch*, *Invercloy*, *Glenrosa* and a private yacht wait for the tide in the canal basin. The nine mile long Crinan Canal enables vessels to avoid the passage round the Mull of Kintyre. The locks take vessels up to 85ft long. Once busy with puffers and sailing coasters the canal is now used mainly by a variety of small craft.

Above: In the days of the coal-burning liner the puffers often had the task of re-stocking bunkers while the discharge of the big ship's cargo went on simultaneously. In this picture assorted puffers are seen servicing the liner *Melita* in 1924. The nearest vessels are former canal mineral scows which finished their days in Princes Dock, Glasgow, supplying steam to portable grain elevators.

Top right: By 1960 the steam driven puffer had ceased to be an economic proposition and many vessels were scrapped. The survivors were converted to motor vessels. The *Kaffir* was among a few which underwent a more elaborate reconstruction which gave a welcome increase of speed and cargo capacity. The *Kaffir*, as a motor vessel, is seen entering Princes Dock.

Right: Puffers on a salvage job at Plantation Quay. In April 1938 the Clyde tug *Flying Spray* was sunk by the propeller of the vessel she was assisting to berth. This photograph shows preparations being made for four of John Hay's puffers to lift her. The *Serb* and *Cretan* are moored over the wreck in mid-stream while *Tartar* and *Dorothy* are at the quay wall.

(John Smith)

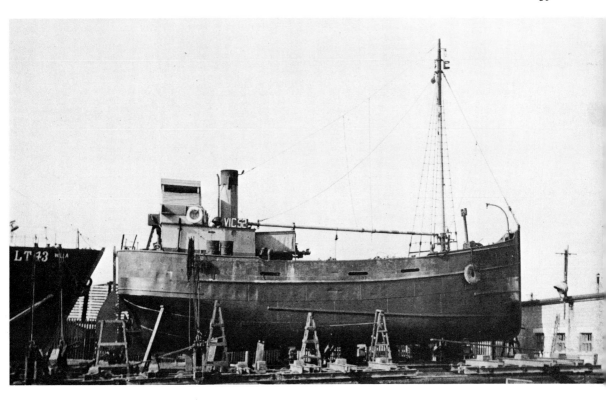

Above: VIC 52 on the slipway showing the underbody. All except two of the *VICs* were built in small English yards. *VIC 52* had been in use as a water tank vessel for the Admiralty.

(Port of Lowestoft Research Society)

Top left: The *Tuscan* of 1935 and the *Lascar* of 1939 offer a comparison in sterns. The former, built at Kirkintilloch, has the type of stern introduced about 1890, and the latter, built for the John Hay fleet by Scott & Sons of Bowling, has the newer type which, though less pleasing to the eye, has more room and buoyancy aft. The *Lascar* was the prototype for the 63 *VIC* type puffers built for the Ministry of War Transport. When this photograph was taken in 1948 the *Tuscan* had just been fitted with a new engine and a new oil-burning boiler. She foundered off Brodick in 1955. The *Lascar* was converted to diesel propulsion in 1959 and was broken up at Troon about 1972.

Left: Lady Isle (No 1) at Port Ascaig, Islay. Built as *VIC 7* by R Dunston at Thorne near Doncaster in 1941 she was purchased by D McCorquodale of Troon. She was wrecked off Scarinish, Tiree in 1956.

Right: Glenaray, ex-*VIC 89*, was built at Thorne in 1944 and was acquired in 1947 by Hamilton & McPhail who spent a considerable amount to bring her up to their standard. She was withdrawn in 1963 and broken up in the following year.

Right: A puffer and a tramcar combine to accent the Victorian atmosphere still preserved by Rothesay, the popular Bute resort, between the wars. The veteran *Elizabeth* of 1866 was one of a small fleet owned by George Halliday, a local timber merchant. Puffers and small sailing craft supplied most of the town's needs in coal and minerals. The *Elizabeth*, largely rebuilt following a stranding in 1895, survived until the second world war.

(Author's collection)

Left: In 1944–5 a second series of *VIC*s was built for the Ministry of War Transport. They were larger than the first series—80ft long and 146 tons gross—and to simplify construction they were built on the straight frame principle. They were not handsome, but they had good accommodation. The *Sir James* was built by Harker & Sons at Knottingly as *VIC 82*. In 1955 she came to the John Hay fleet and was later sold to Ian Dutch of Perth for sand dredging. The photograph shows her in the River Tay at low tide. The oufferman's verdict: not bad boats if they would only steer.

Above: The MV *Innishowen* was one of the vessels introduced by the Coasting Motor Shipping Co of Glasgow to exploit the advantages of the internal combustion engine. Built by Peter MacGregor & Co at Kirkintilloch in 1913, she was 75ft long compared with the 66ft of the earlier vessels in the fleet. Because she was too long for the locks she was taken down the canal in two sections. She was powered by a two cylinder Kromhout hot-bulb oil engine. The experiment was not a success and after the first world war the fleet was dispersed, the *Innishowen* going first to John Summers & Co of Shotton, who lengthened and re-engined her and then in 1947 to Denmark where she became the *Eva Peterson*. *(Author's collection)*

Below: A general view of Ross & Marshall's building and repair yard at Greenock with the *Skylight* of 1879 in the centre.

(Author's collection)

Above: The launch of a puffer. A large crowd turned out to see the *Norman* launched into the canal at John Hay's Kirkintilloch yard in 1895. She joined the Hay fleet. In 1930 she was sold to Rothesay owners and gave 20 years more service before going to the breakers.

(Strathkelvin District Libraries)

Below: The *Rebecca*, *Mary* and *Gartsherrie* were the last of the canal mineral scows. They had begun life as horse drawn barges. Latterly they served as grain elevator barges at Princes Dock and were broken up in 1958.

Above: In 1953 was launched the *Glenshira*, the first motor puffer to join the Clyde fleet since John M Paton's venture of 1912. She was propelled by a five cylinder Polar diesel engine and was fitted with a five ton derrick. She could carry up to 180 tons but still retained the ability to use the Crinan Canal. All hands were quartered aft, the master and engineer having cabins to themselves. A galley, messroom and bathroom were provided. She was owned by Hamilton and McPhail until 1974 when she was sold to P M Herbert of Bude.

Below: For 40 years Walter Kerr's *Saxon*, seen here in the harbour at Millport, Isle of Cumbrae, supplied the island with coal. Built in 1903 by John Hay & Sons as the *Dane*, she was acquired by Walter Kerr having been sunk in a collision in 1925. She appeared as the *Vital Spark* in the BBC Television *Para Handy* series.

(Phil Thomas)

Above: A collision on the Forth & Clyde Canal between a vessel thought to be one of the early Carron Company lighters and the puffer *Lucullite*. The latter was built in 1899 by Ross & Marshall at their Greenock yard, and sold to Warnock Brothers of Paisley in 1919.

(*Strathkelvin District Libraries*)

Below: John Hay & Company's yard at Kirkintilloch in winter with the canal frozen over. In the centre of the picture is the *Moor* while on the right is the *Greek* in the process of being broken up.

Left: The *Goliath* was an iron vessel built by Burrell & Sons at Hamiltonhill in 1878 for their own use. She was 51 tons gross and driven by a single cylinder engine. In the late 1880s she was employed by William Arrol on the construction of the Forth Bridge. She passed to Peter MacGregor of Kirkintilloch and, later, was acquired by owners in Newburgh on the Tay where this picture was taken. About 1920 she went to the Fowey Coaling and Ship Repairing Company and was broken up in 1927.

(Author's collection)

Below left: The puffer's successor — the *Glenfyne*. This 199-ton motor coaster was built in 1965 by Scott & Sons of Bowling. She is thoroughly modern in equipment and accommodation, and can carry 240 tons at a speed of 9½ knots. With her diesel-hydraulic derrick crane she can discharge a grab cargo in a few hours. She is seen here discharging agricultural lime at Toberonochy, Isle of Luing, a former slate quarry harbour.

Right: The puffer *La Belle*, built at Kirkintilloch, was registered in 1893 but is thought to have been working for John Hay & Sons on the Forth & Clyde Canal for a year or two before that. Early in this century she was acquired by the Tayside Floorcloth Company and is seen here at Newburgh, Fife while in their ownership. She had wooden bulwarks added to make her suitable for coastal work. She was replaced about 1924 by a newer vessel.

(Wemyss Craigie)

Below: The *Otter* was built at Paisley in 1886. She is seen in this picture discharging a coal cargo at Easdale, one of several places in Argyllshire which provided a large export of roofing slates for the Clyde and Central Scotland. The *Otter* was lost in bad weather on a passage from Bowling to the Caledonian Canal with coal in September 1892.

(Wemyss Craigie)

The Development of the Puffer

Date of build	Name	Material	Builders and Engine Makers	Gross Tonnage	Dimensions (feet)	Machinery
1857	Glasgow	Iron	Swan & Co Kelvin Dock Fisher & Co	60	63.2 x 17 x 8.3	1 cyl 14″ x 14″ stroke 20NHP
1860	Alpheus	Wood	Wishart & Co Port Glasgow —	52	64.5 x 17.6 x 7.4	2 cyl(2) 10″ x 12″ stroke 50 lbs 18NHP
1866	Sapphire	Iron	A McMillan & Co Dumbarton P. Taylor Falkirk	63	65 x 16.7 x 7.2	1 cyl 10½″ x 12″ stroke 16NHP
1869	Hercules (a)	Iron	Swan & Co Kelvin Dock W King & Co Glasgow	40	66 x 14.4 x 5.5	2 cyl(2) 8″ x 10″ stroke 15NHP
1874	Kenilworth	Iron	Scottish Iron Works Co Irvine Builders	61	65.5 x 18.1 x 7.7	2 cyl(2) 10″ x 15″ stroke 60 lbs 20NHP
1876	Sunlight (b)	Iron	Cumming & Swan Blackhill Kincaid, Donald & Co	44	66.3 x 13.6 x 5.5	1 cyl 10″ x 12″ stroke 20NHP
1880	Lyra	Iron	J & J Hay Kirkintilloch Hutson & Corbett	67	66.2 x 17.4 x 7.7	1 cyl 14½″ x 15″ stroke 20NHP
1884	Terrier (a)	Iron	Burrell & Son Pt Dundas Builders	48	66 x 15.3 x 6	1 cyl 12″ x 12″ stroke 13NHP
1885	John Strachan	Iron	Swan & Co Kelvin Dock Clarkson & Beckett	73	66 x 17.9 x 8.1	1 cyl 15″ x 15″ stroke 23NHP
1893	Gnome	Steel	Marshall & Co Kelvin Dock J Donald & Sons	92	66.2 x 18.2 x 8.7	2 cyl comp 85 IHP 11½″ & 21″ x 15″ stroke
1893	Ashdale Glen	Steel	Burrell & Son Hamiltonhill Fisher & Co Paisley	70	64.6 x 17.5 x 6.9	2 cyl comp 100 lbs p.s.i. 9″ & 18″ x 14″ stroke 13½NHP
1893	Eagle	Iron and Steel	Scott & Sons Bowling Ross & Duncan	90	65.6 x 18.5 x 8.9	2 cyl comp 100IHP 10″ & 20″ x 15″ stroke
1894	Macleod (c)	Steel	Scott & Sons Bowling Walker, Henderson & Co	122	82 x 18.5 x 8.8	2 cyl comp 20NHP 10″ & 20″ x 16″ stroke
1895	Norman	Iron	J & J Hay Kirkintilloch Ross & Duncan	85	65.8 x 18 x 8.4	2 cyl comp 17NHP 11″ & 20″ x 15″ stroke
1901	Dorothy	Steel	Burrell & Son Hamiltonhill Walker, Henderson & Co	99	65.6 x 18.4 x 9.2	2 cyl comp 16NHP 10″ & 20″ x 16″ stroke
1904	Ailsa	Steel	W Denny & Bros Builders	100	66.5 x 18.3 x 8.8	2 cyl comp 7NHP 10″ & 20″ x 16″ stroke
1906	Faithful	Steel	Larne S B Co Larne J D Gauldie Glasgow	95	66.6 x 18.4 x 8.5	2 cyl comp 17NHP 11″ & 20″ x 16″ stroke
1908	Cossack	Steel	J & J Hay Kirkintilloch Builders	92	66.3 x 18.1 x 8.8	2 cyl tandem comp 17NHP 10″ & 21″ x 15″ stroke
1912	Innisagra	Steel	P MacGregor & Co Kirkintilloch Bolinders M/V Stockholm	94	65.6 x 18.4 x 8.7	2 cyl hot bulb oil engine 80BHP
1919	Warlight (c)	Steel	Ross & Marshal Greenock McKie & Baxter Govan	135	86.2 x 18.6 x 9.2	2 cyl comp 24NHP 11½″ & 24″ x 18″ stroke
1921	Starfinch (c)	Steel	P MacGregor & Co Kirkintilloch Gauldie, Gillespie & Co	114	75.2 x 18.6 x 8.9	2 cyl comp 30NHP 10″ & 20″ x 16″ stroke
1930	Sealight (c)	Steel	Geo Brown & Co Greenock Miller & McFie	154	85.5 x 19.6 x 9.2	2 cyl comp 50RHP 12″ & 24″ x 18″ stroke

(a) Canal type
(b) Monkland Canal type
(c) Crinan Canal type